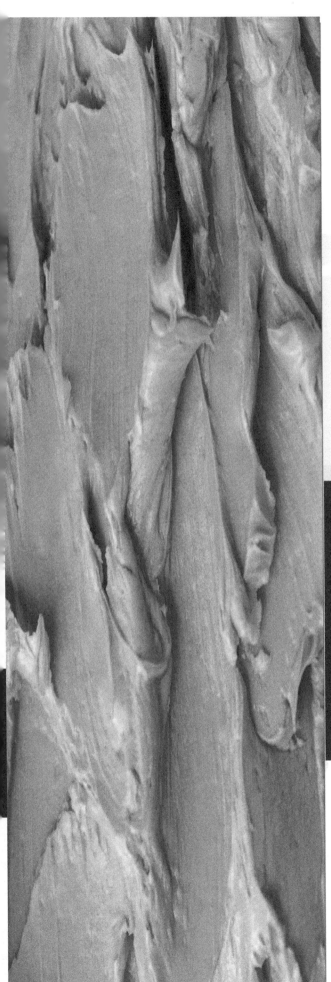

NINJA
CREAMi
COOKBOOK
FOR **BEGINNERS**

Table of content

Chapter- 4: Ice Cream Mix-In   41

Chapter- 5: Sorbet   55

Chapter- 6: MilkShakes   68

Chapter- 7: Smoothie Bowls

Introduction

We can't deny the fact that ice cream is one of the most delicious meals in the whole world. Ice cream is a well-known frozen treat that people all over the world enjoy consuming. Ice cream, with its creamy texture and irresistible flavor, has captivated the attention of people for many years and remains a top favorite across all age groups. It's possible to make ice cream using a wide variety of components, such as milk, sugar, eggs, chocolate powder, and vanilla extract. The ice cream's special texture, taste, and appearance are all the result of the combination of these various ingredients.

With the Ninja CREAMi, you can produce ice cream just as creamy and tasty as homemade ice cream, but instead of storing it in the freezer, you can easily make it on your kitchen counter without making a mess! You don't need to freeze your treats in a big freezer, which saves both space and money.

Due to its user-friendly design and wide range of applications, the Ninja® CREAMi™ has transformed the world of homemade ice cream and other frozen desserts. This simple device is fun to use, and you do not need any technical equipment to do so. You can have the best ice cream, Sorbet, Ice cream mix-ins, Smoothie bowls, Milkshake, and Gelato as long as you have some measuring spoons, cups, a freezer, and a Ninja® CREAMi™. This will ensure that everyone around you has a delicious time. The Ninja CREAMi needs a very small amount of ingredients and occupies very little space on your kitchen counter. In this cookbook, you'll learn how to create all your favorite treats ranging from ice cream, Sorbet, Ice cream mix-ins, Smoothie bowls, milkshakes, and then Gelato from scratch. The unique recipes that can be found in the Ninja CREAMi Cookbook are both family-friendly and delicious.

Chapter 1

Getting Started with the Ninja® CREAMi™

You need to know the functions of the machine before making a move to make ice cream. The Ninja® CREAMi™ is not a very complex piece of equipment, yet it is extremely powerful and has a wide variety of uses. This chapter will provide everything you need to know about CREAMi as well as how to choose the feature that will work best for your own recipes and tastes. You will also learn how to operate and maintain this machine in order to ensure that it will keep producing ice cream and frozen delicacies for many years to come.

You'll be able to get the best value out of this amazing home appliance if you follow the tips that are provided in the guide. After that, take the CREAMi out of its packaging, check each component, clean and dry all the parts, and try to put the machine together. Last but not least, finish reading this chapter, choose a recipe, and start producing the frozen treats you've been looking forward to.

Ninja® CREAMi™ IS NOT ONLY A DEVICE FOR MAKING ICE CREAM

You might get the impression that you have a brand-new ice cream maker when you first open the package containing your Ninja® CREAMi™. Since making ice cream is only one of many things that this machine is capable of doing, in addition to smoothie bowls, gelato, milkshakes, and sorbet, The Ninja® CREAMi™ produces frozen desserts.

When the CREAMi team examined the products already on the market, they reached the conclusion that there was a need for a device that could do more than merely freeze and aerate custard. As a result, they developed this machine. In order to produce a milkshake as a sweet treat, you will need to combine the necessary components in a food processor. Some of these ingredients include milk and mix-ins. The Ninja® CREAMi™, on the other hand, let you mix your ingredients in the pint jar before processing them.

You can fully control the ingredients that go in and out of your CREAMi device when you make your own frozen treats at home. Your CREAMi pints may be personalized to your likes and tastes, whether it involves using fruits or vegetables to increase the amount of nutrition they contain or strictly adhering to recipes that meet your dietary requirements.

Let's check out some of the particular features and advantages of the Ninja® CREAMi™ that highlight exactly how unique and useful this appliance is.

- QUICK PROCESS TIME

It just takes a few minutes for the Ninja® CREAMi™ to complete the processing once the ice cream recipe has been frozen. The frozen ice cream recipe is churned by the CREAMi, which breaks up ice crystals to produce the silkiest, creamiest ice cream, sorbet, and gelato possible.

- SMALLER PROCESS TIME

Due to the lower batch size provided by this device, you won't have to take up as much space in your freezer with a large ice cream container. Simply buy more pint containers and then have a tasting party or ice cream social, including as different flavors as you can handle!

- SIMPLE TO PRODUCE A VARIETY OF FLAVORS

Produce one vanilla base, and then find it easier coming up with two, three, or five other flavors. Ice Cream, Sorbet, and Light ice cream in their various modes

You can produce ice cream, gelato, sorbet, and even lite ice cream by pressing the button. In order to get a creamy texture with sorbets and smoothie bowls, you will need to process them for a longer time at high speed. You don't need to make any wild assumptions since the machine takes care of everything for you, regardless of what you want to produce.

- MAKE-AHEAD FUNCTION AND FEATURE

You can prepare as many different kinds of ice cream in advance as you want and then just store them in the freezer until you need them. When you are ready to enjoy it, put the base in the Ninja® CREAMi processor.

- EASY TO MAINTAIN AND CLEAN

Except for the part containing the Dual Drive Motor, every component of the Ninja® CREAMi™ can be safely cleaned in the dishwasher using the top rack. Ninja® CREAMi™ dishwasher, you may easily clean the components by hand using soap and warm water.

1.1 FUNCTIONS OF NINJA CREAMi

1. Ice Cream

This device is specially made for foods that are conventionally considered to be indulgent. It is ideal for converting dairy and dairy-free food into ice creams that are smooth, creamy, and thick enough to be scooped.

2. Lite Ice Cream

This device has been deliberately developed for those concerned about their health to successfully prepare low-fat, low-sugar, or sugar-free alternatives to ice cream.

3. Gelato

This device was intended primarily for use with custard bases, more especially for ice creams (Italian-style). It works particularly well when the recipe centers on a mouthwatering and delicious dessert.

4. Sorbet

This device has been specially designed to transform fruit-heavy recipes that need a lot of water and sugar into delicious creamy delights.

5. Milkshake

This device is designed to produce thick milkshakes in a very short amount of time. Simply add your preferred mix-ins, ice cream, and milk to the milkshake maker. Pressing the milkshake button will have the milkshake ready for you in a short amount of time.

6. Smoothie Bowl

This device was developed with the purpose of making it easier to prepare dishes that demand fresh or frozen fruits, vegetables, juice, dairy substitutes, or dairy products in addition to other ingredients.

7. Mix-In

This device's primary objective is to fully fold any bits of nuts, frozen fruits, sweets, cereal, or cookies that have been added in order to personalize a treat that has been bought or a base that has just been prepared.

8. Re-Spin

This device has been designed to provide a smooth and fine texture after successfully implementing either of the preset features.

1.2 Features of the Ninja CREAMi

The Ninja CREAMi frozen treat maker has so many features that make it the best device for reducing ice cream costs.

1. Creamerizer Paddle
2. CREAMi Pint Lid
3. Outer Bowl
4. Outer Bowl Lid
5. 16 oz. CREAMi Pint
6. Motor Base

To begin, the Ninja CREAMi offers functions that are easy to use. The device has what's known as a one-click soft start, which means that once you plug it in, it won't instantly start by itself. Rather, it has a delayed start, which enables the machine to switch on gently without shocking you with unexpected noise or vibration caused by rapid initiation.

There is also an automatic shut-off timer that starts counting down after sixty minutes. Since it has an automatic shut-off function, the Ninja machine can also be used at night without the user having to worry about turning it off before going to bed. This is different from other products now available on the market.

This Ninja machine is the first and only ice cream maker that is equipped with a dedicated electronic weight display. Since it weighs the components as they are added, you can rest assured that the total quantity of each component will always be correct and constant. As a result of this, it is well suitable for use in commercial settings as well as at home production since one family member will be able to produce a particular quantity of ice cream.

This Ninja device comes with a freezer bowl that can be removed anytime, allowing you to prepare a frozen dessert mix or a recipe for soft-serve ice cream. If you remove the bowl from the machine, you will be able to move it from one place to another without any unnecessary difficulty and in a considerably shorter amount of time. In case you find it difficult to find your bowl when it is required, the device comes with a set of storage bags that make it simple to keep the bowl in the freezer when it is not in use.

The Ninja CREAMi is equipped with a cutting blade made of stainless steel, and its purpose is to shatter the ice crystals that are responsible for the delicious creaminess of ice cream. Since it comes with an automated stirrer as well as an agitator paddle, there can't be any unpleasant mixing and stirring. Since this device is equipped with a multi-stage automated timer as well as a temperature control system, you will always be able to achieve the ideal consistency! In addition, the cover is transparent, so you can watch your frozen treat being churned without taking your eyes off of it.

The Ninja CREAMi also has a design that makes it uncomplicated to clean, which enables it to be cleaned quickly and efficiently. You can quickly clean this machine without too much effort when you use a brush with bristles made from premium nylon. This brush makes the task of wiping down the machine much simpler. In addition to that, the device has a bowl that can be removed and is also safe to clean in the dishwasher. With the help of this portable device, you won't have to stress about cleaning up any of the messes that result from making desserts.

Lastly, the Ninja CREAMi is a lightweight and portable home appliance. The appliance weighs about twelve pounds and can be placed on top of the countertops in most kitchens without restricting access to other appliances or taking up excessive space. It has dimensions of 11.8 inches by 8.8 inches by 4.5 inches.

1.3 MAIN INGREDIENTS OF NINJA CREAMi

One of the most top-notch benefits of using the Ninja® CREAMiTM is that it gives you full control over the recipes that go into your frozen desserts. The ingredients in this book have been subjected to rigorous testing and have been standardized to guarantee continuous improvement. When substituting recipes, particularly as you get more familiar with your CREAMi, you need to be careful since the end product may not live up to your expectations. Since this book has a wide variety of recipes, it doesn't matter what kind of diet you maintain or what kinds of foods you can't eat—you'll still be able to find something delicious here to make.

The following are the main ingredients that are used most often in CREAMi meals.

1. **Milk That Is Not Made From Dairy**
People who are lactose intolerant have access to a variety of high-quality milk alternatives. Among these are quinoa milk, oat milk, hemp milk, rice milk, cashew milk, and other nut milk like cashew milk and macadamia nut milk. Most of these components are mostly lightweight and do not provide an unusual taste to the frozen treats.

2. **Dairy**
Quite a few of the frozen desserts in this book extensively use various dairy ingredients. There are several wonderful alternatives to choose from, including skim or 1 percent milk, 2 percent milk, whole milk, heavy (whipping) cream, light cream, cream cheese, and even yogurt.

3. **Chocolate combined with cocoa powder.**
Chocolate can be purchased in a wide range of forms, including blocks, chips, powder, wafers, and bars. There is also the possibility of using chocolate syrup or chocolate milk. The classification of chocolate is based on the percentage of cocoa content, which refers to pure chocolate that has undergone just minimal processing. The quantity of cocoa in the chocolate will increase as it gets darker, and no sugar will be added.

4. Eggs.

Fresh eggs are an important ingredient in many ice cream and gelato recipes; eggs that are spotless and unbroken are always the best. In addition, to ensure your wellbeing, the egg custard ice cream bases you use should always be boiled as specified in the recipe.

5. Sweeteners apart from general sugar.

A number of different sweeteners, including maple syrup, dates, molasses, agave nectar, coconut sugar, and fruit, are often used in the production of ice cream and sorbets. Use components of the best quality you can purchase while taking note of their expiry dates. Since sugar is essential to the structure and taste of ice cream, it is not suggested that honey or molasses be used in place of granulated sugar unless the recipe specifically instructs otherwise. Honey and molasses have a different flavor profiles than sugar.

In comparison, semisweet chocolate normally has between 50 and 60 percent cacao, whereas dark chocolate has between 60 and 70 percent cacao. White chocolate can't be referred to as chocolate since it does not have any solid chocolate, although milk chocolate has the least amount of cacao of any kind of chocolate.

It is possible to make chocolate out of cocoa powder if a sufficient amount of fat is added.

6. Extracts, flavorings, and alcohol.

Any kind of alcoholic treat can't be frozen. Since alcohol lowers the freezing point of whatever it is added to, ice cream prepared with rum has a smoother texture than traditional ice cream.

7. Extracts and flavorings significantly impact the final product when it comes to ice cream recipes.

Make sure you use a vanilla extract of the top-notch grade along with other spices. Look for companies that use Madagascar vanilla beans since these are considered among the top ones. Add a split vanilla bean to your vanilla extract container for a richer taste. Other flavors that may be extracted include mint, peppermint, maple, almond, banana, lemon, lime, orange, butter, coconut, and anise.

1.4 F.A.Qs

Here's a top list of the most frequently asked questions and answers about this appliance from previous customers.

1. What made the ice cream have such a dry and crumbly texture after it was processed?

There is a possibility that the base was at an extremely low temperature. Re-assemble the device, then press the button labeled "Re-Spin." As a result of this, the base may be processed for a longer amount of time, which will result in a smoother overall experience. The amount of sugar or fat in your recipe may be too low. Make use of the provided recipes as a guide to get the best possible outcomes.

2. How much of each mix-in should I add to each CREAMi pint?

It is advisable to use a V* cup of mix-ins for every pint of ice cream. If you are using different mix-ins, you should not add more than V* cups worth of total mix-ins to your pint.

3. Do you think I can use my pint containers to fill the machine?

No, because the CREAMi Pint containers are specifically made to have a tight fit inside the machine, using any other containers may be hazardous.

4. How do you feel about making substitutions?

These recipes were tested over the years using the Ninja® CREAMi™ appliance. If you are not directed by a recommendation, replacing one or two components with anything else might lead to a tragic incident.

5. How many servings of ice cream can the Ninja Creami make at a time?

The Ninja Creami is capable of producing frozen treats in containers with a capacity of one pint, and the machine itself comes with three containers with a capacity of three pints. Also, Ninja offers additional pint containers that can be bought at any store.

6. Once the ice cream has been prepared in the CREAMi, is it possible to freeze it?

Yes, you can. Put the storage top that comes with the CREAMi Pint on the CREAMi Pint, and then set it in the freezer. Before you consume your previously-saved ice cream, you must first return it to the CREAMi and put it via the software that was used throughout the production process.

7. If I want to make a CREAMi Pint, how many bases should I use?

There is a fill line that is specified on the side of each CREAMi Pint container; ensure not to fill the container more than halfway.

Chapter

2

Ice Cream

Vanilla ice cream

INTERMEDIATE RECIPE

NUTRITION

Calories: 96

Protein: 6g

Carbohydrate: 18g

Fat: 0.1g

Sodium: 156mg

SHOPPING LIST

- 1 cup of cold milk
- ½ teaspoon of vanilla essence
- ¼ tablespoon of corn flour
- ¼ cup of sugar
- ¼ cup of fresh cream

DIRECTIONS

1. Prepare a smooth paste in a small bowl by combining corn flour and milk. If you do not use cold milk, there will be lumps. Add all the necessary ingredients into a bowl and set them aside. Combine the remaining milk, sugar, and vanilla extract in a mixing bowl.
2. Transfer the mixture to a clean and empty ninja CREAMi Pint container, and then place it in the freezer for 24 hrs.
3. Take the pint out of the freezer after twenty-four hours. Take off the cover.
4. Transfer the Ninja CREAMi Pint to the outer bowl of the device. Turn the ninja CREAMi machine so that the outer bowl is locked into position once you have placed it inside the machine with the pint already within it, then push the "Ice Cream" button.
5. When the ICE CREAM operation is complete, turn the outer bowl and remove it from the device.

10
MINUTES

1

Mango ice cream

INTERMEDIATE RECIPE

📖 NUTRITION

Calories: 96

Protein: 6g

Carbohydrate: 18g

Fat: 0.1g

Sodium: 156mg

🧺 SHOPPING LIST

- 1 mango (medium-sized, cut into quarters)
- 1 cup of milk
- 1 tablespoon of cream cheese (room temperature)
- ¼ cup of sugar
- ¾ cup of heavy whipping cream

🛍️ DIRECTIONS

1. Mix the sugar and cream cheese in a mixing bowl. Stir with a whisk until all the ingredients are evenly distributed, and the sugar begins to dissolve.
2. Pour the milk and heavy whipping cream into the bowl, and stir with a whisk until they are well combined.
3. Pour the mixture into a new CREAMi Pint container that has been cleaned out. After pouring the mango into the pint, place it in the freezer for 24 hours. You need to ensure that the amount of fruit does not exceed the maximum fill line.
4. After the pint has spent 24 hours in the freezer, take it out. Remove the protective cover.
5. Put the Ninja CREAMi Pint into the outer bowl. Adjust the ninja CREAMi machine so that the outer bowl is locked into position once you have placed it inside the machine with the pint already in it, then press the "ICE CREAM" button. The ice cream will be stirred and made into a very smooth texture while the ICE CREAM function is performed.
6. When the ICE CREAM function of the ninja CREAMi machine is completed, rotate the outer bowl and remove it from the device.

10
MINUTES

1

Coffee ice cream

INTERMEDIATE RECIPE

NUTRITION

Calories:230

Protein:1.1g

Carbohydrate: 33.8g

Fat: 11.2g

SHOPPING LIST

- 1½ tablespoons of instant coffee powder
- 1 cup of rice milk
- 1 teaspoon of vanilla extract
- ½ cup of granulated sugar
- ¾ cup of coconut cream

DIRECTIONS

Coconut cream should be stirred in a bowl until it is completely smooth.

Add all the remaining ingredients, then continue stirring until the sugar has completely dissolved.

Pour the mixture into an empty pint-sized Ninja CREAMi container.

Put the lid on the storage container, then place it in the freezer for 24 hours.

After a period of twenty-four hours, remove the lid and pour the mixture into the outer bowl of the Ninja CREAMi.

Attach the Creamerizer Paddle to the outer bowl lid.

After that, turn the lid in a clockwise direction to lock it.

To turn on the machine, press the "power" button.

After that, press the "Ice Cream" button.

After the device has finished running, you will need to rotate the Outer Bowl and then

remove it from the machine.

Pour the ice cream into different serving cups, and serve it as soon as possible.

10
MINUTES

4

Chocolate & Spinach Ice Cream

INTERMEDIATE RECIPE

NUTRITION

Calories: 243

Carbohydrates: 36.7g

Protein: 3.4g

Fat: 10.1g

Sodium: 55mg.

SHOPPING LIST

- 1 cup of whole milk
- ½ cup of frozen spinach, thawed and squeezed dry
- 1 tsp. of mint extract
- ½ cup of granulated sugar
- 3-5 drops of green food coloring

- 1/3 cup of heavy cream
- ¼ cup of chocolate chunks, chopped
- ¼ cup of brownie, cut into 1-inch pieces

DIRECTIONS

1. Add the sugar, mint extract, food coloring, spinach, and milk in a blender with a high-speed setting, then blend the ingredients until the mixture is completely smooth.

2. Pour the mixture inside a Ninja CREAMi pint container that has been cleaned and emptied.

3. Pour in the heavy cream and stir until it is completely mixed.

4. Place the storage lid on top of the container, and place it in the freezer for 24 hours.

5. After twenty-four hours, take the lid off the container and pour the mixture inside the Ninja CREAMi's outer bowl.

6. Place the "Creamerizer Paddle" onto the top of the outer bowl after it has been covered.

7. After that, lock the lid by turning it clockwise, then press the "Power" button. 9. Press the "ICE CREAM" button.

8. When the process is finished, use a spoon to make a hole in the center of the pint jar that is 1.5 inches wide. Let the hole reach the bottom of the pint container.

9. Add the chocolate chunks and brownie pieces into the hole created, and press the "MIX-IN" button.

10. Once the device has finished running, rotate the outer bowl and remove it from the machine.

11. Pour the ice cream into individual serving bowls and serve it as soon as possible.

10 MINUTES

2

Strawberry ice cream

INTERMEDIATE RECIPE

NUTRITION

Calories:175
Fat:10.5g
Carbohydrates:18.8g
Protein: 2.8g

SHOPPING LIST

- 6 medium fresh strawberries, hulled and quartered
- 1 tablespoon of cream cheese, softened
- 1 teaspoon of vanilla bean paste
- 1 cup of milk
- ¼ cup of sugar
- ¾ cup of heavy whipping cream

DIRECTIONS

1. Add the cream cheese, sugar, and vanilla bean paste to a bowl and use a wire whisk to mix the ingredients until they are smooth.
2. After adding the milk and heavy whipping cream, continue mixing until it is completely blended.
3. Pour the mixture into a pint container of Ninja CREAMi that has been left unfilled.
4. Add the strawberry pieces, then give the mixture a thorough stir.
5. Put the filled container in the freezer for 24 hours with the storage cover on top.
6. Take the cover from the container and pour the mixture into the outer bowl of the Ninja CREAMi.
7. Place the creamerizer paddle on the cover of the outer bowl.
8. To secure the lid, turn it clockwise.
9. Press the "Power" button.
10. After that, press the "Ice Cream" button
11. Once the machine has finished running, rotate the outer bowl and then remove it from the device.
12. Pour the ice cream into individual serving dishes and serve it as soon as possible.

10
MINUTES

4

Cherry-chocolate Chunk Ice Cream

INTERMEDIATE RECIP

NUTRITION

Calories: 458
Protein: 7.2g
Carbohydrate: 48g
Fat: 28g
Sodium: 92mg

SHOPPING LIST

- 1 cup whole cherries pitted
- 1 can of sweetened condensed milk
- 1 teaspoon of vanilla extract
- 1 bar of semisweet baking chocolate, broken into small chunks
- ½ cup of milk
- ¾ cup of heavy cream

DIRECTIONS

1. Add the heavy cream, sweetened condensed milk, and milk together with the vanilla extract in a bowl.
2. Transfer the ice cream to an unfilled ninja CREAMi Pint container, then stir in the chocolate chunks and chopped cherries, and place the container in the freezer for 24 hrs.
3. Take out the container from the freezer and also remove the cover.
4. Transfer the Ninja CREAMi Pint to the outer bowl of the blender. Rotate the ninja CREAMi machine so that the outer bowl is locked into position. Press the "ICE CREAM" button.
5. Once the process is done, rotate the outer bowl and remove it from the device.

10 MINUTES

4

Chocolate Ice Cream

INTERMEDIATE RECIPE

NUTRITION

Calories: 96
Protein: 6g
Carbohydrate: 18g
Fat: 0.1g
Sodium: 156mg

SHOPPING LIST

- ½ can of sweetened condensed milk
- ½ cup of unsweetened cocoa powder
- ½ teaspoon of vanilla extract
- ¾ cup of heavy whipping cream

DIRECTIONS

1. Mix the cocoa powder, sweetened condensed milk, and vanilla extract in a medium-scale bowl.
2. Stir the heavy cream in an empty bowl until it has the texture of soft peaks (do not over-stir).
3. Transfer the mixture to a ninja CREAMi Pint container that has been cleaned thoroughly, and then freeze it for 24 hrs.
4. Take out the container from the freezer and remove the cover.
5. Transfer the Ninja CREAMi Pint to the outer bowl of the mixing container. Rotate the ninja CREAMi machine so that the outer bowl is locked into position. Press the "Ice Cream" button. During the ICE CREAM process, the ice cream will combine and turn into a highly creamy texture.
6. When the ICE CREAM function of the ninja CREAMi machine is complete, rotate the outer bowl and then remove it from the device.

10
MINUTES

1

Caramel Ice Cream

INTERMEDIATE RECIPE

 NUTRITION

Calories: 897
Protein: 15.11g
Fat: 42.34g
Carbs: 111.94g

 SHOPPING LIST

- 14 oz. of canned dulce de leche
- 1 ¼ cups of heavy cream
- 1 tablespoons of bourbon

DIRECTIONS

1. Place all the ingredients into an electric mixer's mixing bowl.
2. Continue mixing until the mixture becomes thicker.
3. Pour the ingredients into the pint container that came with your Ninja Creami.
4. Place in a freezer for eight hours.
5. Place the container into the machine.
6. Press the "Ice cream" button.
7. Finally, serve

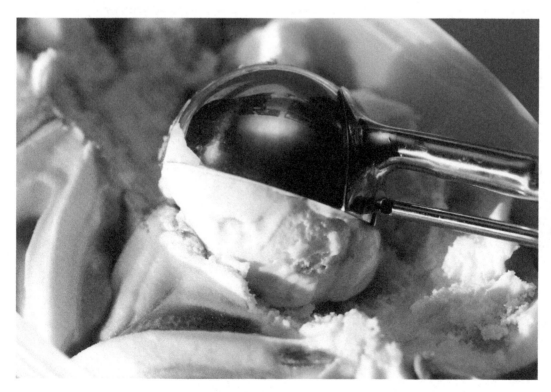

15 MINUTES

2

Peanut Butter Ice Cream

INTERMEDIATE RECIPE

📖 NUTRITION

Calories: 143
Protein: 6.5g
Carbohydrates:19.7g
Fats: 6.1g

🧺 SHOPPING LIST

- 3 tablespoons of smooth peanut butter
- 1¾ cups of skim milk
- ¼ cup of stevia-cane sugar blend
- 1 teaspoon of vanilla extract

🛍 DIRECTIONS

1. Add all necessary ingredients into a container and mix with a hand mixer until smooth.
2. Set the bowl aside for approximately five minutes.
3. Pour the mixture into a pint container of Ninja CREAMi that is empty.
4. Put the container in the freezer for 24 hours with the storage lid on top.
5. Take out the lid from the container and place the mixture inside the Ninja CREAMi's outer bowl.
6. Place the creamerizer paddle on top of the outer bowl's lid.
7. Finally, to secure the lid, turn it clockwise.
8. Press the "Power" button.
9. After that, press the "Ice Cream" button.
10 Once the device has finished running, rotate the outer bowl and then remove it from the machine.
11. Pour the ice cream into individual serving bowls and serve it as soon as possible.

10 MINUTES

4

Lemon Ice Cream

INTERMEDIATE RECIPE

NUTRITION

Calories: 280
Protein: 1.5g
Carbohydrates: 28.2g
Fats: 18.3g

SHOPPING LIST

- 1 (14-ounce) can of full-Fats: unsweetened coconut milk
- 1 teaspoon of vanilla extract
- 1 teaspoon of lemon extract
- ½ cup of granulated sugar

DIRECTIONS

1. Pour the coconut milk into a bowl and stir it until it is completely smooth.
2. After adding the remaining ingredients, continue stirring the mixture until the sugar is completely dissolved.
3. Pour the mixture into a pint container of Ninja CREAMi that has been left unfilled.
4. Put the container in the freezer for 24 hours with the storage cover on top.
5. Take the cover off the container and pour the ingredients into the outer bowl of the Ninja CREAMi.
6. Place the creamerizer paddle on the cover of the outer bowl.
7. Finally, to secure the lid, turn it clockwise.
8. Press the "Power" button.
9. Once the device has finished running, turn the outer bowl and then remove it from the machine.
10. Pour the ice cream into individual serving cups and serve it as soon as possible.

10 MINUTES

4

Fruity Extract Ice Cream

INTERMEDIATE RECIPE

NUTRITION

Calories: 115
Protein: 3.1g
Carbohydrates: 19.4g
Fats: 4g

SHOPPING LIST

- 1 cup of whole milk
- ¾ cup of heavy cream
- 2 tablespoons of monk fruit sweetener with erythritol
- 2 tablespoons of agave nectar
- ½ teaspoon of raspberry extract

- ½ teaspoon of vanilla extract
- ¼ teaspoon of lemon extract
- 5-6 drops of blue food coloring

DIRECTIONS

1. Add all the necessary ingredients in a bowl and mix them well.
2. Place the ingredients inside a Ninja CREAMi pint container that has been cleaned and emptied.
3. Put the filled container in the freezer for 24 hours with the storage cover on top.
4. Take the cover off the container and pour the mixture into the Ninja CREAMi's outer bowl.
5. Place the "Creamerizer Paddle" on top of the outer bowl's cover.
6. Finally, to secure the lid, turn it clockwise.
7. Press the "Power" button and then the "ICE CREAM" button.
8. After that, you need to hit the "ICE CREAM" button.
9. When the device has finished running, turn the outer bowl and then remove it from the machine.
10. Place the ice cream in individual serving dishes, and serve it as soon as possible.

10 MINUTES

4

Cherry Ice Cream

INTERMEDIATE RECIPE

NUTRITION

Calories: 1251
Protein: 26.95g
Fat: 36.85g
Carbs: 203.52g

SHOPPING LIST

- ½ cup of dark cherries, sliced in half
- ⅓ cup of instant pudding mix
- ½ cup of half and half cream
- 1 ½ cups of milk
- 3 tablespoons of chocolate chips

DIRECTIONS

1. Add all necessary ingredients into a bowl, excluding the chocolate chips, then stir thoroughly.
2. Transfer the mixture to the pint container of the Ninja Creami.
3. Place it in a freezer for 24 hours.
4. Set the container in the device.
5. Select the "Ice Cream" button.
6. Add the little chocolate chips.
7. Select the Mix-in mode from the menu.

20 MINUTES

1

Green Tea Ice Cream

INTERMEDIATE RECIPE

NUTRITION

Calories: 188
Fat: 11.2g
Carbohydrates:20.3g
Protein: 2.6g

SHOPPING LIST

- ½ cup of granulated sugar
- 1 tablespoon of cream cheese
- 2 tablespoons of vanilla extract
- 1½ tablespoons of green tea (matcha) powder
- 1 cup of milk
- ¾ cup of heavy cream

DIRECTIONS

1. Place the cream cheese in the microwave for ten seconds, then stir until the mixture is smooth.
2. Combine the softened cream cheese, sugar, green tea powder, and vanilla essence, and whisk the mixture thoroughly.
3. Pour the milk and cream into the mixture and stir until they've blended.
4. Pour the mixture into a clean and empty Ninja CREAMi Pint.
5. Put the lid on the filled container, and place it in the freezer for 24 hours.
6. Take off the top and place the pint inside the larger bowl of the Ninja CREAMi.
7. Place the Creamerizer Paddle into the machine, and then lock the lid.
8. Press the "Ice Cream" button.
9. When the device has finished running, turn the outer bowl and then remove it from the device.
10: Serve in dishes for individual consumption.

10 MINUTES

4

Frozen Hot Chocolate Ice Cream

NUTRITION

Calories: 355
Protein: 10.84g
Fat: 8.32g
Carbs: 63.65g

INTERMEDIATE RECIPE

SHOPPING LIST

- 1 cup of chocolate milk
- ¼ cup of cream
- ¼ cup of almond milk creamer
- 1 oz. of hot cocoa mix

DIRECTIONS

1. Combine the chocolate milk and cream.
2. Give it a thorough mix.
3. Heat it for two minutes in the microwave.
4. Add the hot cocoa.
5. Transfer the mixture from the mixing bowl to the Ninja Creami pint container.
6. Place in the refrigerator for 10 minutes.
7. Mix well, then place in the freezer for 24 hours.
8. Transfer the container to the machine.
9. Press the "Ice Cream" button.

20 MINUTES

2 MINUTES

1

Coconut Ice Cream

INTERMEDIATE RECIPE

NUTRITION

Calories: 406
Protein: 3g
Carbohydrate 36g
Fat 29g
Sodium 86mg

SHOPPING LIST

- ½ cup of milk
- 1 can cream of coconut
- ¾ cup of heavy cream
- ½ cup of sweetened flaked coconut

DIRECTIONS

1. Add the coconut milk and coconut cream into the blender and process until completely blended.
2. Mix the heavy cream and flaked coconut in another bowl, then pour this mixture into the bowl containing the milk and cream. Mix thoroughly.
3. Transfer the mixture to a clean and empty ninja CREAMi Pint container, then place it in the freezer for 24 hours.
4. Take the pint out of the freezer after twenty-four hours and remove the cover.
5. Transfer the Ninja CREAMi Pint to the outer bowl. After placing the outer bowl together with the pint into the Ninja CREAMi machine, rotate the device until the outer bowl is fixed in its position.
6. Turn the outer bowl clockwise and remove it from the Ninja CREAMi machine after the ICE CREAM process is complete.

10
MINUTES

4

Chapter 3

Gelato

Triple Chocolate Gelato

DIRECTIONS

1. Mix the cocoa powder, sugar, egg yolks, and chocolate fudge together in a small saucepan.
2. Continue stirring the mixture after adding the milk and heavy cream.
3. Heat the mixture while constantly stirring for approximately two to three minutes.
4. Stop heating, then add and stir the chocolate pieces until they are fully melted.
5. Pour the mixture into an empty Ninja CREAMi pint container using a fine-mesh strainer.
6. To cool the container, place it in an ice bath.
7. After cooling, cover the container and place it in the freezer for 24 hours.
8. Remove the cover and place it in the Ninja CREAMi's outer bowl.
9. Attach the "Creamerizer Paddle" to the outer bowl's cover.
10. Press the "Power" button.
11. After that, press the "GELATO" button.
12. Serve the gelato.

SHOPPING LIST

- 4 large egg yolks
- 1/3 cup of dark brown sugar
- 2 tbsp. of dark cocoa powder
- 1 tbsp. of chocolate fudge topping
- ¾ cup of heavy cream
- ¾ cup of whole milk
- 2-3 tbsp. of chocolate chunks, chopped

NUTRITION

Calories: 256

Carbohydrates:22.8g

Protein: 5.8g

Fat: 16.7g

Sodium: 59mg.

5 MINUTES

3 MINUTES

4

Carrot Gelato

BASIC RECIPE

 DIRECTIONS

1. Mix the coconut sugar, brown rice syrup, and egg yolks together in a small saucepan.
2. Continue stirring the mixture after adding the spices, almond milk, carrot puree and heavy cream.
3. Heat the mixture while constantly stirring for approximately two to three minutes.
4. Stop heating, then add vanilla extract.
5. Pour the mixture into an empty Ninja CREAMi pint container using a fine-mesh strainer.
6. To cool the container, place it in an ice bath.
7. After cooling, cover the container and place it in the freezer for 24 hours.
8. Remove the cover and place it in the Ninja CREAMi's outer bowl.
9. Attach the "Creamerizer Paddle" to the outer bowl's cover.
10. Press the "Power" button.
11. After that, press the "GELATO" button.
12. Serve the gelato.

SHOPPING LIST

- 3 large egg yolks
- 1/3 cup of coconut sugar
- 1 tbsp. of brown rice syrup
- ½ cup of heavy cream
- 1 cup of unsweetened almond milk
- ½ cup of carrot puree
- ½ tsp. of ground cinnamon
- ¼ tsp. of ground nutmeg
- ¼ tsp. of ground ginger
- ¼ tsp. of ground cloves
- ¾ tsp. of vanilla extract

NUTRITION

Calories: 146
Carbohydrates:22.7g
Protein: 0.8g
Fat: 6.5g
Sodium: 64mg.

5 MINUTES

3 MINUTES

4

Pistachio Gelato

BASIC RECIPE

 DIRECTIONS

1. Combine the sugar, egg yolks, and corn syrup in a small saucepan and stir until the ingredients are well combined.
2. Stir in the almond extract, heavy cream, milk, and food coloring.
3. Set the pan over a medium heat source. Cook using a rubber spatula to stir continuously until an instant-read thermometer reads 165°F to 175°F.
4. Transfer the base into a clean CREAMi Pint after passing it through a fine-mesh strainer. Make sure the water doesn't leak into the base when you carefully set the container in the ice water bath.
5. After the base has cooled, cover it and place it in freeze for 24 hours. Remove the pint cover and take it out of the freezer. Put the pint in the Ninja CREAMi's outer bowl, put the Creamerizer Paddle in the lid, and attach the cover assembly to the outer bowl. Choose the Gelato option.
6. Remove the cover from the pint container when the process is complete. Make a hole with a spoon that is 1½-inch-wide and also gets the pint's bottom. Fill the pint's hole with the pistachios, and then choose the Mix-In option.
7. Take the gelato out of the pint after the process is complete. Serve right away.

 **SHOPPING LIST**

- 4 large egg yolks
- ¼ cup of plus 1 tablespoon granulated sugar
- 1 tablespoon of light corn syrup
- ⅓ cup of whole milk
- 1 cup of heavy (whipping) cream
- 1 teaspoon of almond extract
- 5 drops of green food coloring
- ¼ cup of roasted pistachios

 NUTRITION

Calories: 222
Carbohydrates: 21g
Protein: 2g
Fat: 14g
Sodium: 105mg.

 5 MINUTES

 10 MINUTES

 4

Sweet Potato
Gelato

BASIC RECIPE

 DIRECTIONS

1. Mix the sweet potato puree, egg yolks, sugar, ½ teaspoon of cinnamon, and nutmeg together in a small saucepan.
2. Continue stirring the mixture after adding the heavy cream and vanilla extract.
3. Heat the mixture while constantly stirring for approximately two to three minutes.
4. Pour the mixture into an empty Ninja CREAMi pint container using a fine-mesh strainer.
5. To cool the container, place it in an ice bath.
6. After cooling, cover the container and place it in the freezer for 24 hours.
7. Remove the cover and put the pint in the Ninja CREAMi's outer bowl, put the Creamerizer Paddle in the lid, and attach the cover assembly to the outer bowl. Press the "Power" button.
8. After that, press the "GELATO" button.
9. Serve the gelato.

 SHOPPING LIST

- ½ cup of canned sweet potato puree
- 4 large egg yolks
- ¼ cup of sugar
- ½ tsp. of ground cinnamon
- 1/8 tsp. of ground nutmeg
- 1 cup of heavy cream
- 1 tsp. of vanilla extract

 NUTRITION

Calories: 239
Carbohydrates: 21.5g
Protein: 4g
Fat: 15.7g
Sodium: 44mg.

5 MINUTES

3 MINUTES

4

Strawberry Cheesecake Gelato

BASIC RECIPE

DIRECTIONS

1. Combine the sugar and egg in a small saucepan and stir until the ingredients are well combined.
2. Stir in the vanilla, heavy cream, milk, cream cheese, and strawberry.
3. Set the mixture saucepan over a medium heat source. Cook using a rubber spatula to stir continuously until an instant-read thermometer reads 165°F to 175°F.
4. Transfer the base into a clean CREAMi Pint after passing it through a fine-mesh strainer. Make sure the water doesn't leak into the base when you carefully set the container in the ice water bath.
5. After the base has cooled, cover and place it in freeze for 24 hours. Remove the pint cover and take it out of the freezer. Put the pint in the Ninja CREAMi's outer bowl, put the Creamerizer Paddle in the lid, and attach the cover assembly to the outer bowl. Choose the Gelato option.
6. Remove the cover from the pint container when the process is complete. Make a hole with a spoon that is 1½-inch-wide and also gets the pint's bottom. Fill the pint's hole with the graham cracker, and then choose the Mix-In option.
7. Take the gelato out of the pint after the process is complete. Serve right away.

NUTRITION

Calories: 130
Carbohydrates: 21g
Protein: 4g
Fat: 4.5g
Sodium: 55mg.

SHOPPING LIST

- FUNCTIONS: Gelato and Mix-In
- TOOLS NEEDED: Large bowl, small saucepan, whisk, rubber spatula, instant-read thermometer, fine-mesh strainer, spoon
- 4 large egg yolks
- 3 tablespoons of granulated sugar
- 1 cup of whole milk
- ⅓ cup of heavy (whipping) cream
- ¼ cup of cream cheese, at room temperature
- 1 teaspoon of vanilla extract
- 3 tablespoons strawberry jam
- ¼ cup graham cracker pieces

4

10 MINUTES

5 MINUTES

Red Velvet Gelato

BASIC RECIPE

 DIRECTIONS

1. Combine the egg yolks, sugar, and cocoa powder in a small saucepan and stir until the ingredients are well combined.
2. Stir in the vanilla, heavy cream, milk, cream cheese, and food coloring.
3. Set the mixture saucepan over a medium heat source. Cook using a rubber spatula to stir continuously until an instant-read thermometer reads 165°F to 175°F.
4. Transfer the base into a clean CREAMi Pint after passing it through a fine-mesh strainer. Make sure the water doesn't leak into the base when you carefully set the container in the ice water bath.
5. After the base has cooled, cover it and place it in freeze for 24 hours. Remove the pint cover and take it out of the freezer. Put the pint in the Ninja CREAMi's outer bowl, put the Creamerizer Paddle in the lid, and attach the cover assembly to the outer bowl. Choose the Gelato option.
6. Take the gelato out of the pint after the process is complete. Serve right away.

 SHOPPING LIST

- 4 large egg yolks
- ¼ cup of granulated sugar
- 2 tablespoons of unsweetened cocoa powder
- 1 cup of whole milk
- ⅓ cup heavy (whipping) cream
- ¼ cup of cream cheese, at room temperature
- 1 teaspoon of vanilla extract
- 1 teaspoon of red food coloring

 NUTRITION

Calories: 170
Carbohydrates: 17g
Protein: 1g
Fat: 7g
Sodium: 65mg.

5 MINUTES

10 MINUTES

4

Pumpkin Gelato

BASIC RECIPE

DIRECTIONS

1. Mix the sugar, egg yolks, and corn syrup together in a small saucepan.
2. Continue stirring the mixture after adding the heavy cream, milk, pumpkin pie spice and pumpkin puree.
3. Heat the mixture while constantly stirring for approximately two to three minutes.
4. Stop heating, then add vanilla extract.
5. Pour the mixture into an empty Ninja CREAMi pint container using a fine-mesh strainer.
6. To cool the container, place it in an ice bath.
7. After cooling, cover the container and place it in the freezer for 24 hours.
8. Remove the pint cover and take it out of the freezer. Put the pint in the Ninja CREAMi's outer bowl, put the Creamerizer Paddle in the lid, and attach the cover assembly to the outer bowl.
9. Press the "Power" button.
10. After that, press the "GELATO" button. Serve the gelato.

 SHOPPING LIST

- 3 large egg yolks
- 1/3 cup of granulated sugar
- 1 tbsp. of light corn syrup
- 1 cup of whole milk
- ½ cup of heavy cream
- ½ cup of canned pumpkin puree
- 1½ tsp. of pumpkin pie spice
- 1 tsp. of vanilla extract

NUTRITION

Calories: 220
Carbohydrates: 27g
Protein: 4.7g
Fat: 11.1g
Sodium: 39mg.

5 MINUTES

3 MINUTES

4

Chocolate-hazelnut Gelato

BASIC RECIPE

 DIRECTIONS

1. Combine the sugar, egg yolks, chocolate-hazelnut spread, cocoa powder, and corn syrup in a small saucepan and mix until the ingredients are well combined.

2. Stir in the heavy cream, milk, and vanilla.
3. Set the mixture saucepan pan over a medium heat source. Cook using a rubber spatula to stir continuously until an instant-read thermometer reads 165°F to 175°F.

4. Transfer the base into a clean CREAMi Pint after passing it through a fine-mesh strainer. Make sure the water doesn't leak into the base when you carefully set the container in the ice water bath.

5. After the base has cooled, cover it and place it in freeze for 24 hours. Remove the pint cover and take it out of the freezer. Put the pint in the Ninja CREAMi's outer bowl, put the Creamerizer Paddle in the lid, and attach the cover assembly to the outer bowl. Choose the Gelato option.

6. Take the gelato out of the pint after the process is complete. Serve right away.

 SHOPPING LIST

- 3 large egg yolks
- ⅓ cup of chocolate-hazelnut spread
- 2 teaspoons of unsweetened cocoa powder
- 1 tablespoon of corn syrup
- ¼ cup of granulated sugar
- 1 cup of whole milk
- ½ cup of heavy (whipping) cream
- 1 teaspoon of vanilla extract

 NUTRITION

Calories: 170
Carbohydrates: 19g
Protein: 2g
Fat: 9g
Sodium: 20mg.

5 MINUTES

10 MINUTES

4

Squash Gelato

BASIC RECIPE

 DIRECTIONS

1. Mix all the necessary ingredients together in a small saucepan.
2. Continue stirring the mixture over medium heat for approximately 5 minutes.
3. Put the mixture in an empty Ninja CREAMi pint container.
4. To cool the container, place it in an ice bath.
5. After cooling, cover the container and place it in the freezer for 24 hours.
6. Remove the cover and place it in the Ninja CREAMi's outer bowl.
7. Attach the "Creamerizer Paddle" to the outer bowl's cover.
8. Press the "Power" button.
9. After that, press the "GELATO" button.
10. Serve the gelato.

 NUTRITION

Calories: 109
Carbohydrates: 20.1g
Protein: 3.7g
Fat: 2.2g
Sodium: 90mg.

 **SHOPPING LIST**

- 1¾ cup of milk
- ½ cup of cooked butternut squash
- ¼ cup of granulated sugar
- ½ tsp. of ground cinnamon
- ¼ tsp. of ground allspice
- Pinch of salt

5 MINUTES

5 MINUTES

4

Chocolate Cauliflower Gelato

BASIC RECIPE

 DIRECTIONS

1. Mix all ingredients except chopped chocolate together in a small saucepan.
2. Heat the mixture while constantly stirring for approximately two to three minutes.
3. Transfer the base into a clean CREAMi Pint after passing it through a fine-mesh strainer. Make sure the water doesn't leak into the base when you carefully set the container in the ice water bath.
4. After the base has cooled, cover it and place it in freeze for 24 hours. Remove the pint cover and take it out of the freezer. Put the pint in the Ninja CREAMi's outer bowl, put the Creamerizer Paddle in the lid, and attach the cover assembly to the outer bowl. Choose the Gelato option.
5. Remove the cover from the pint container when the process is complete. Make a hole with a spoon that is 1½-inch-wide and also gets the pint's bottom.
6. Fill the pint's hole with the chopped chocolate, and then choose the Mix-In option.
7. Take the gelato out of the pint after the process is complete. Serve right away.

 SHOPPING LIST

- 1 cup of whole milk
- ½ cup of heavy cream
- 1/3 cup of sugar
- 2 tbsp. of cocoa powder
- ½ cup of frozen cauliflower rice
- ¼ tsp. of almond extract
- Pinch of salt
- ½ cup of dark chocolate, chopped

 NUTRITION

Calories: 273
Carbohydrates: 34.5g
Protein: 4.6g
Fat: 14.1g
Sodium: 90mg.

5 MINUTES

3 MINUTES

4

Tiramisu Gelato

BASIC RECIPE

 DIRECTIONS

1. Combine the sugar and egg in a small saucepan and stir until the ingredients are well combined.

2. Stir in the instant coffee, cream cheese, heavy cream, milk, and rum extract.

3. Set the pan over a medium heat source. Cook using a rubber spatula to stir continuously until an instant-read thermometer reads 165°F to 175°F.

4. Transfer the base into a clean CREAMi Pint after passing it through a fine-mesh strainer. Make sure the water doesn't leak into the base when you carefully set the container in the ice water bath.

5. After the base has cooled, cover it and place it in freeze for 24 hours. Remove the pint cover and take it out of the freezer. Put the pint in the Ninja CREAMi's outer bowl, put the Creamerizer Paddle in the lid, and attach the cover assembly to the outer bowl. Choose the Gelato option.

6. Remove the cover from the pint container when the process is complete. Make a hole with a spoon that is 1½-inch-wide and also gets the pint's bottom. Fill the pint's hole with the ladyfinger pieces, and then choose the Mix-In option.

7. Take the gelato out of the pint after the process is complete. Serve right away.

 SHOPPING LIST

- 4 large egg yolks
- ⅓ cup of granulated sugar
- 1 cup of whole milk
- ⅓ cup of heavy (whipping) cream
- ¼ cup of cream cheese
- 1 tablespoon of instant coffee
- 1 teaspoon of rum extract
- ¼ cup of ladyfinger pieces

 NUTRITION

Calories: 140
Carbohydrates: 14g
Protein: 4g
Fat: 6g
Sodium: 50mg.

5 MINUTES

10 MINUTES

4

Banana & Squash Cookie Gelato

BASIC RECIPE

 DIRECTIONS

1. Mix egg yolks, heavy cream, and sugar together in a small saucepan.
2. Heat the mixture while constantly stirring for approximately two to three minutes.
3. Transfer the base into a clean CREAMi Pint after passing it through a fine-mesh strainer. Make sure the water doesn't leak into the base when you carefully set the container in the ice water bath, then add squash, pudding, and squash.
4. After the base has cooled, cover it and place it in freeze for 24 hours. Remove the pint cover and take it out of the freezer. Put the pint in the Ninja CREAMi's outer bowl, put the Creamerizer Paddle in the lid, and attach the cover assembly to the outer bowl. Choose the Gelato option.
5. Remove the cover from the pint container when the process is complete. Make a hole with a spoon that is 1½-inch-wide and also gets the pint's bottom.
6. Fill the pint's hole with the wafer cookies, and then choose the Mix-In option.
7. Take the gelato out of the pint after the process is complete. Serve right away.

 NUTRITION

Calories: 489
Carbohydrates: 61.6g
Protein: 5.7g
Fat: 24.7g
Sodium: 194mg.

SHOPPING LIST

- 4 large egg yolks
- 1 cup of heavy cream
- 1/3 cup of granulated sugar
- ½ of banana, peeled and sliced
- ½ cup of frozen butternut squash, chopped
- 1 box instant vanilla pudding mix
- 6 vanilla wafer cookies, crumbled

5 MINUTES

3 MINUTES

4

Chapter 4

ICE CREAM

MIX-IN

Mint Cookies
Ice Cream

BASIC RECIPES

NUTRITION

Calories: 201

Fat: 12.8g

Protein: 2.4g

Carbohydrates: 21.9g

SHOPPING LIST

- ¾ cup of coconut cream
- ¼ cup of monk fruit sweetener with Erythritol
- 2 tablespoons of agave nectar
- ½ teaspoon mint extract
- 5-6 drops green food coloring
- 1 cup of oat milk
- 3 chocolate sandwich cookies, quartered

DIRECTIONS

1. Add the coconut cream to a big bowl and whisk it until it's creamy.
2. Combine and stir the sweetener, mint extract, agave nectar, and food coloring.
3. Add the oat milk and mix well.
4. Pour the mixture into a pint-sized Ninja CREAMi container that is empty.
5. Place a storage cover on the container and place it in the freezer for 24 hours.
6. Remove the cover and put the pint in the Ninja CREAMi's outer bowl.
7. Attach the Creamerizer Paddle to the outer bowl's cover.
8. Next, lock the lid by turning it clockwise.
9. Press the "Power" button, then press "Lite Ice Cream.
10. After the device has finished running, use a spoon to make a hole in the middle that is 1½-inch wide and extends all the way to the bottom of the pint container.
11. Fill the hole with the cookie pieces and press the "Mix-In" button.
12. Turn the outer bowl and remove it from the machine.
13. Serve right away.

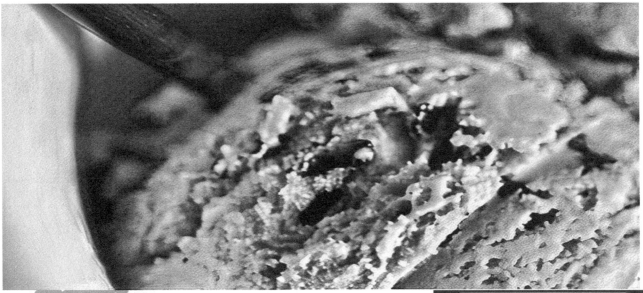

Coffee Chip Ice Cream

INTERMEDIATE RECIPE

 NUTRITION

Calories 145   Protein 1.8g

Fat 12.7g

Carbohydrates 6.1g

 DIRECTIONS

1. Add the heavy cream to a big bowl and whisk it until it's smooth.
2. Add and stir the monk fruit, stevia sweetener, coffee, almond milk, and vanilla extract.
3. Pour the mixture into a pint-sized Ninja CREAMi container that is empty.
4. Place a storage cover on the container and place it in the freezer for 24 hours.
5. Remove the cover and Put the pint in the Ninja CREAMi's outer bowl.
6. Attach the Creamerizer Paddle to the outer bowl's cover.
7. Next, lock the lid by turning it clockwise.
8. Press the "Power" button, then press "Lite Ice Cream."
9. After the device has finished running, use a spoon to make a hole in the middle that is 1½-inch wide and extends all the way to the bottom of the pint container.
10. Fill the hole with the walnuts and chocolate chips and press the "Mix-In" button.
11. Turn the outer bowl and remove it from the machine.
12. Serve right away.

 SHOPPING LIST

- ¾ cup heavy cream
- ¼ cup monk fruit sweetener with Erythritol
- ½ teaspoon stevia sweetener
- 1½ tablespoons instant coffee granules
- 1 cup unsweetened almond milk
- 1 teaspoon vanilla extract
- 3 tablespoons chocolate chips
- 1 tablespoon walnuts, chopped

10 MINUTES

4

Chocolate-covered Coconut And Almond Ice Cream

BASIC RECIPES

 NUTRITION

Calories: 260

Fat: 17g

Carbohydrates: 24g

Protein: 4g

 DIRECTIONS

1. Combine and stir the sugar, coconut milk, almond milk, and vanilla.
2. Pour the mixture into a pint-sized Ninja CREAMi container that is empty.
3. Place a storage cover on the container and place it in the freezer for 24 hours.
4. Remove the cover and put the pint in the Ninja CREAMi's outer bowl.
5. Attach the Creamerizer Paddle to the outer bowl's cover.
6. Next, lock the lid by turning it clockwise.
7. Press the "Power" button, then press the "Ice Cream" button.
8. After the device has finished running, use a spoon to make a hole in the middle that is 1½-inch wide and extends all the way to the bottom of the pint container.
9. Fill the hole with the almond halves and chocolate chips and press the "Mix-In" button.
10. Turn the outer bowl and remove it from the machine.
11. Serve right away.

 **SHOPPING LIST**

- TOOLS NEEDED: Medium bowl, whisk, spoon
- 1 can full-fat unsweetened coconut milk
- ¼ cup of unsweetened almond milk
- ½ cup of organic sugar
- 1 teaspoon of vanilla extract
- 2 tablespoons of toasted almond halves
- 2 tablespoons of vegan chocolate chips

4

10
MINUTES

Sneaky Mint Chip Ice Cream

BASIC RECIPES

NUTRITION

Calories: 201

Fat: 12.8g

Carbohydrates: 21.9g

Protein: 2.4g

DIRECTIONS

1. Combine the egg, corn syrup, and sugar in a small saucepan and stir until the ingredients are well combined.
2. Stir in the heavy cream and milk.
3. Set the pan over a medium heat source. Cook using a rubber spatula to stir continuously until an instant-read thermometer reads 165°F to 175°F.
4. Transfer the base into a clean CREAMi Pint after passing it through a fine-mesh strainer. Make sure the water doesn't leak into the base when you carefully set the container in the ice water bath.
5. After the mixture has been allowed to fully cool, pour it into a blender and add the spinach, peas, and mint extract. Blend the ingredients for 30 seconds at the highest speed. After passing it through a filter with a fine screen, pour the base into the CREAMi Pint. Cover the container with its storage cover, then place it in the freezer for 24 hours.
6. Remove the cover and Put the pint in the Ninja CREAMi's outer bowl. Attach the Creamerizer Paddle to the outer bowl's cover, then lock the lid by turning it clockwise.
7. Press the "Power" button, then press the "Ice Cream" button.
8. After the device is finished running, use a spoon to make a hole in the middle that is 1½-inch wide and extends all the way to the bottom of the pint container. Fill the hole with the chocolate chips and press the "Mix-In" button.
9. Turn the outer bowl and remove it from the machine. Serve right away.

🧺 SHOPPING LIST

- 3 large egg yolks
- 1 tablespoon of corn syrup
- ¼ cup of granulated sugar
- ⅓ cup of whole milk
- ¾ cup of heavy (whipping) cream
- 1 cup of packed fresh spinach
- ½ cup of frozen peas, thawed
- 1 teaspoon of mint extract
- ¼ cup of semisweet chocolate chips

Chocolate Brownie

Ice Cream

BASIC RECIPES

SHOPPING LIST

- 1 tablespoon of cream cheese, softened
- ⅓ cup of granulated sugar
- 1 teaspoon vanilla extract
- 2 tablespoons of cocoa powder
- 1 cup of whole milk
- ¾ cup of heavy cream
- 2 tablespoons of mini chocolate chips
- 2 tablespoons of brownie chunks

 NUTRITION

Calories: 232

Fat: 13.7g

Protein: 3.6g

Carbohydrates: 25.9g

 DIRECTIONS

1. Microwave the cream cheese for 10 seconds.
2. Whisk until it is smooth after removing the cream cheese from the microwave
3. Add the sugar and almond extract to a big bowl and whisk it until it's smooth.
4. Add and stir the milk and heavy cream.
5. Pour the mixture into a pint-sized Ninja CREAMi container that is empty.
6. Place a storage cover on the container and place it in the freezer for 24 hours.
7. Remove the cover and Put the pint in the Ninja CREAMi's outer bowl.
8. Attach the Creamerizer Paddle to the outer bowl's cover.
9. Next, lock the lid by turning it clockwise.
10. Press the "Power" button, then press the "Ice Cream" button.
11. After the device has finished running, use a spoon to make a hole in the middle that is 1½-inch wide and extends all the way to the bottom of the pint container.
12. Fill the hole with the chocolate chunks and brownie pieces and press the "Mix-In" button.
13. Turn the outer bowl and remove it from the machine.
14. Serve right away.

10 SECONDS

4

10 MINUTES

Coffee And Cookies

Ice Cream

BASIC RECIPES

NUTRITION

Calories: 150

Fat: 8g

Carbohydrates: 19g

Protein: 2g

SHOPPING LIST

- 1 tablespoon of cream cheese, at room temperature
- ⅓ cup of granulated sugar
- 1 teaspoon vanilla extract
- 1 tablespoon of instant espresso
- ¾ cup heavy (whipping) cream
- 1 cup of whole milk
- ¼ cup of crushed chocolate sandwich cookies

DIRECTIONS

1. Combine and stir the cream cheese, sugar, and vanilla for about 1 minute.
2. Add and stir the instant espresso, heavy cream, and milk until completely combined.
3. Pour the mixture into a pint-sized Ninja CREAMi container that is empty.
4. Place a storage cover on the container and place it in the freezer for 24 hours.
5. Remove the cover and put the pint in the Ninja CREAMi's outer bowl.
6. Attach the Creamerizer Paddle to the outer bowl's cover.
7. Next, lock the lid by turning it clockwise.
8. Press the "Power" button, then press "Ice Cream" button.
9. After the device has finished running, use a spoon to make a hole in the middle that is 1½-inch wide and extends all the way to the bottom of the pint container.
10. Fill the hole with the almond halves and chocolate chips and press the "Mix-In" button.
11. Turn the outer bowl and remove it from the machine.
12. Serve right away.

1 MINUTES

4

10 MINUTES

Rocky Road Ice Cream

BASIC RECIPES

 SHOPPING LIST

- 1 cup of whole milk
- ½ cup of frozen cauliflower florets, thawed
- ½ cup of dark brown sugar
- 3 tablespoons of dark cocoa powder
- 1 teaspoon of chocolate extract
- ⅓ cup of heavy cream
- 2 tablespoons of almonds, sliced
- 2 tablespoons of mini marshmallows
- 2 tablespoons of mini chocolate chips

 NUTRITION

Calories: 202

Fat: 9.3g

Carbohydrates: 28.7g

Protein: 4.2g

 DIRECTIONS

1. Add the milk, cauliflower, brown sugar, cocoa powder, and chocolate extract into a blender, then blend.
2. Pour the mixture into a pint-sized Ninja CREAMi container that is empty, then add the heavy cream.
3. Place a storage cover on the container and place it in the freezer for 24 hours.
4. Remove the cover and put the pint in the Ninja CREAMi's outer bowl.
5. Attach the Creamerizer Paddle to the outer bowl's cover.
6. Next, lock the lid by turning it clockwise.
7. Press the "Power" button, then press the "Ice Cream" button.
8. After the device has finished running, use a spoon to make a hole in the middle that is 1½-inch wide and extends all the way to the bottom of the pint container.
9. Fill the hole with the almond halves, marshmallows, and chocolate chips, and press the "Mix-In" button.
10. Turn the outer bowl and remove it from the machine.
11. Serve right away.

4

10
MINUTES

Snack Mix Ice Cream

BASIC RECIPES

NUTRITION

Calories: 182

Protein: 3.6g

Fat: 4.3g

Carbohydrates: 32.8g

SHOPPING LIST

- 1 tablespoon of cream cheese, softened
- ⅓ cup of granulated sugar
- ½ teaspoon of vanilla extract
- 1 cup of whole milk
- ¾ cup of heavy cream
- 2 tablespoons of sugar cone pieces
- 1 tablespoon of mini pretzels
- 1 tablespoon of potato chips, crushed

DIRECTIONS

1. Microwave the cream cheese for 10 seconds.
2. Whisk in the vanilla extract and sugar until it is smooth after removing the cream cheese from the microwave
3. Slowly add and stir the milk and heavy cream.
4. Pour the mixture into a pint-sized Ninja CREAMi container that is empty.
5. Place a storage cover on the container and place it in the freezer for 24 hours.
6. Remove the cover and Put the pint in the Ninja CREAMi's outer bowl.
7. Attach the Creamerizer Paddle to the outer bowl's cover.
8. Next, lock the lid by turning it clockwise.
9. Press the "Power" button, then press the "Ice Cream" button.
10. After the device has finished running, use a spoon to make a hole in the middle that is 1½-inch wide and extends all the way to the bottom of the pint container.
11. Fill the hole with the cone pieces, pretzels, and potato chips, and press the "Mix-In" button.
12. Turn the outer bowl and remove it from the machine.
13. Serve right away.

10 SECONDS

4

10 MINUTES

Coconut Mint Chip

Ice Cream

BASIC RECIPES

SHOPPING LIST

- 1 can full-fat unsweetened coconut milk
- ½ cup of organic sugar
- ½ teaspoon of mint extract
- ¼ cup of mini vegan chocolate chips

NUTRITION

Calories: 180

Fat: 11g

Carbohydrates: 17g

Protein: 1g

DIRECTIONS

1. Combine the coconut milk, sugar, and mint extract.
2. Pour the mixture into a pint-sized Ninja CREAMi container that is empty.
3. Place a storage cover on the container and place it in the freezer for 24 hours.
4. Remove the cover and put the pint in the Ninja CREAMi's outer bowl.
5. Attach the Creamerizer Paddle to the outer bowl's cover.
6. Next, lock the lid by turning it clockwise.
7. Press the "Power" button, then press the "Ice Cream" button.
8. After the device has finished running, use a spoon to make a hole in the middle that is 1½-inch wide and extends all the way to the bottom of the pint container.
9. Fill the available hole with the mini chocolate chips and press the "Mix-In" button.
10. Turn the outer bowl and remove it from the machine.
11. Serve right away.

4

10
MINUTES

Bourbon-maple-walnut

Ice Cream

BASIC RECIPES

 SHOPPING LIST

- 4 large egg yolks
- ¼ cup of maple syrup
- ¼ cup of corn syrup
- 2 tablespoons of bourbon
- ½ cup of whole milk
- 1 cup of heavy (whipping) cream
- ¼ cup of toasted walnut halves

 DIRECTIONS

1. Combine the egg yolks, maple syrup, corn syrup, and bourbon in a small saucepan and stir until the ingredients are well combined.
2. Stir in the milk and heavy cream.
3. Set the pan over a medium heat source. Cook using a rubber spatula to stir continuously until an instant-read thermometer reads 165°F to 175°F.
4. Transfer the base into a clean CREAMi Pint.
Make sure the water doesn't leak into the base when you carefully set the container in the ice water bath.
5. After the base has cooled, cover it and place it in freeze for 24 hours. Remove the pint cover and take it out of the freezer. Put the pint in the Ninja CREAMi's outer bowl, put the Creamerizer Paddle in the lid, and attach the cover assembly to the outer bowl. Press the "Ice Cream" button.
6. Remove the cover from the pint container when the process is complete. Make a hole with a spoon that is 1½-inch-wide and also gets the pint's bottom. Fill the pint's hole with the toasted walnuts, and then choose the Mix-In option.
7. Take the gelato out of the pint after the process is complete. Serve right away.

10 MINUTES

4

10 MINUTES

Sweet Potato Pie

Ice Cream

BASIC RECIPES

 NUTRITION

Calories: 201

Fat: 12.8g

Protein: 2.4g

Carbohydrates: 21.9g

 DIRECTIONS

1. Combine the sweet potato puree, corn syrup, brown sugar, vanilla, and cinnamon, and blend.
2. Pour the mixture into a pint-sized Ninja CREAMi container that is empty.
3. Place a storage cover on the container and place it in the freezer for 24 hours.
4. Remove the cover and put the pint in the Ninja CREAMi's outer bowl.
5. Attach the Creamerizer Paddle to the outer bowl's cover.
6. Next, lock the lid by turning it clockwise.
7. Press the "Power" button, then press the "Ice Cream" button.
8. After the device has finished running, use a spoon to make a hole in the middle that is 1½-inch wide and extends all the way to the bottom of the pint container.
9. Fill the hole with the marshmallows and press the "Mix-In" button.
10. Turn the outer bowl and remove it from the machine.
11. Serve right away.

 SHOPPING LIST

- 1 cup of canned pureed sweet potato
- 1 tablespoon of corn syrup
- ¼ cup of plus 1 tablespoon light brown sugar
- 1 teaspoon of vanilla extract
- 1 teaspoon of cinnamon
- ¾ cup of heavy (whipping) cream
- ¼ cup of mini marshmallows

SHOPPING LIST

- 3 tablespoons of granulated sugar
- 4 large egg yolks
- 1 cup of whole milk
- ⅓ cup of heavy cream
- ¼ cup of smooth peanut butter
- 3 tablespoons of grape jelly
- ¼ cup of honey roasted peanuts, chopped

Jelly & Peanut Butter

 Ice Cream

BASIC RECIPES

NUTRITION

Calories: 349

Fat: 23.1g

Protein: 11.5g

Carbohydrates: 27.5g

DIRECTIONS

1. Combine the sugar and egg in a small saucepan and stir until the ingredients are well combined.
2. Stir in the milk, heavy cream, peanut butter, and grape jelly.
3. Set the pan over a medium heat source. Cook using a rubber spatula to stir continuously until an instant-read thermometer reads 165°F to 175°F.
4. Transfer the base into a clean CREAMi Pint after passing it through a fine-mesh strainer. Make sure the water doesn't leak into the base when you carefully set the container in the ice water bath.
5. After passing it through a filter with a fine screen, pour the base into the CREAMi Pint. Cover the container with its storage cover, then place it in the freezer for 24 hours.
6. Remove the cover and Put the pint in the Ninja CREAMi's outer bowl. Attach the Creamerizer Paddle to the outer bowl's cover, then lock the lid by turning it clockwise.
7. Press the "Power" button, then press the "Ice Cream" button.
8. After the device is finished running, use a spoon to make a hole in the middle that is 1½-inch wide and extends all the way to the bottom of the pint container. Fill the hole with the peanuts and press the "Mix-In" button.
9. Turn the outer bowl and remove it from the machine. Serve right away.

10 MINUTES

5 MINUTES

4

Lavender Cookie Ice Cream

BASIC RECIPES

 **NUTRITION**

Calories: 229

Fat: 13.2g

Protein: 5g

Carbohydrates: 23.5g

10 MINUTES

SHOPPING LIST

- ¾ cup of heavy cream
- 1 tablespoon of dried culinary lavender
- 1/8 teaspoon of salt
- ¾ cup of whole milk
- ½ cup of sweetened condensed milk
- 4 drops of purple food coloring
- ⅓ cup of chocolate wafer cookies, crushed

 DIRECTIONS

1. Combine the heavy cream, lavender, and salt in a small saucepan and stir until the ingredients are well combined, then place it on low heat for 10 minutes (stir every two minutes).
2. Transfer the base into a clean CREAMi Pint after passing it through a fine-mesh strainer, then discard the lavender leaves.
3. Add and stir the condensed milk, milk, and purple food coloring in the cream mixture bowl.
4. Pour the base into the CREAMi Pint. Cover the container with its storage cover, then place it in the freezer for 24 hours.
5. Remove the cover and Put the pint in the Ninja CREAMi's outer bowl. Attach the Creamerizer Paddle to the outer bowl's cover, then lock the lid by turning it clockwise.
6. Press the "Power" button, then press the "Ice Cream" button.
7. After the device is finished running, use a spoon to make a hole in the middle that is 1½-inch wide and extends all the way to the bottom of the pint container. Fill the hole with the crushed cookies and press the "Mix-In" button.
8. Turn the outer bowl and remove it from the machine. Serve right away.

4

10 MINUTES

Chapter 5

SORBET

Peach Sorbet

BASIC RECIPE

10 MINUTES

4

DIRECTIONS

1. Combine the seltzer and agave, and mix.
2. Put the peaches in an empty Ninja CREAMi pint container, then fill the rest of the container with the seltzer.
3. Place a storage cover on the container and place it in the freezer for 24 hours.
4. Remove the cover and put the pint in the Ninja CREAMi's outer bowl.
5. Attach the Creamerizer Paddle to the outer bowl's cover.
6. Next, lock the lid by turning it clockwise.
7. Press the "Power" button, then press the "Sorbet" button.
8. Turn the outer bowl and remove it from the machine.
9. Serve right away.

SHOPPING LIST

- 1 cup passionfruit seltzer
- 3 tablespoons agave nectar
- 1 can peaches in heavy syrup, drained
-

NUTRITION

Calories: 271

Fat: 1.5g

Protein: 5.3g

Carbohydrates: 65.4g

Pineapple Rum Sorbet

INTERMEDIATE RECIPE

10 MINUTES

4

DIRECTIONS

1. Combine all necessary ingredients in a blender and blend.
2. Put the mixture in an empty Ninja CREAMi pint container.
3. Place a storage cover on the container and place it in the freezer for 24 hours.
4. Remove the cover and put the pint in the Ninja CREAMi's outer bowl.
5. Attach the Creamerizer Paddle to the outer bowl's cover.
6. Next, lock the lid by turning it clockwise.
7. Press the "Power" button, then press the "Sorbet" button.
8. Turn the outer bowl and remove it from the machine.
9. Serve right away.

NUTRITION

Calories: 102

Fat: 0.2g

Carbohydrates: 17.6g

Protein: 0.6g

Sodium: 1mg

SHOPPING LIST

- ¾ cup of piña colada mix
- ¼ cup of rum
- 2 tbsp. of granulated sugar
- 1½ cup of frozen pineapple chunks

Blueberry & Pomegranate Sorbet

INTERMEDIATE RECIPE

DIRECTIONS

1. Put the blueberries in an empty Ninja CREAMi pint container and top with syrup.
2. Stir in pomegranate juice.
3. Place a storage cover on the container and place it in the freezer for 24 hours.
4. Remove the cover and put the pint in the Ninja CREAMi's outer bowl.
5. Attach the Creamerizer Paddle to the outer bowl's cover.
6. Next, lock the lid by turning it clockwise.
7. Press the "Power" button, then press the "Sorbet" button.
8. Turn the outer bowl and remove it from the machine.
9. Serve right away.

NUTRITION

Calories: 101

Fat: 0.4g

Carbohydrates: 25.2g

Protein: 0.8 g

Sodium: 4mg

10 MINUTES

4

SHOPPING LIST

- 1 can blueberries in light syrup
- ½ Cup of pomegranate juice

Lime Sorbet

DIRECTIONS

1. Combine all necessary ingredients in a blender and blend. Set the mixture aside for just 5 mins.
2. Put the mixture in an empty Ninja CREAMi pint container.
3. Place a storage cover on the container and place it in the freezer for 24 hours.
4. Remove the cover and put the pint in the Ninja CREAMi's outer bowl.
5. Attach the Creamerizer Paddle to the outer bowl's cover.
6. Next, lock the lid by turning it clockwise.
7. Press the "Power" button, then press the "Sorbet" button.
8. Turn the outer bowl and remove it from the machine.
9. Serve right away.

NUTRITION

Calories: 69   Protein 0.2 g

Fat: 0g

Carbohydrates: 14.4g

SHOPPING LIST

- ¾ cup of beer
- ⅔ cup of water
- ½ cup of fresh lime juice
- ¼ cup of granulated sugar

Cherry-berry Rosé Sorbet

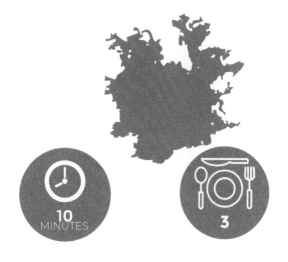

DIRECTIONS

1. Combine all necessary ingredients in a bowl and mix.
2. Put the mixture in an empty Ninja CREAMi pint container.
3. Place a storage cover on the container and place it in the freezer for 24 hours.
4. Remove the cover and put the pint in the Ninja CREAMi's outer bowl.
5. Attach the Creamerizer Paddle to the outer bowl's cover.
6. Next, lock the lid by turning it clockwise.
7. Press the "Power" button, then press the "Sorbet" button. This process should take up to 2 mins
8. Turn the outer bowl and remove it from the machine.
9. Serve right away.

10 MINUTES

3

NUTRITION

Calories: 186

Fat: 0.2g

Carbohydrates: 40g

Protein 1.5g

Sodium: 4.9mg

🧺 SHOPPING LIST

- 2 cups of frozen cherry-berry fruit blend
- ½ cup of rosé wine, or as needed
- ¼ cup of white sugar, or to taste
- ¼ medium lemon, juiced

Orange Sorbet

DIRECTIONS

1. Put the orange pieces in an empty Ninja CREAMi pint container. Let the orange pieces reach the MAX FILL line, then cover it with liquid from the can.
2. Place a storage cover on the container and place it in the freezer for 24 hours.
3. Remove the cover and put the pint in the Ninja CREAMi's outer bowl.
4. Attach the Creamerizer Paddle to the outer bowl's cover.
5. Next, lock the lid by turning it clockwise.
6. Press the "Power" button, then press the "Sorbet" button.
7. Turn the outer bowl and remove it from the machine.
8. Serve right away.

SHOPPING LIST

- 1 can mandarin oranges with liquid

NUTRITION

Calories: 52

Fat: 0g

Carbohydrates: 13.6g

Protein 0.9g

Sodium: 7mg

Pear Sorbet

 DIRECTIONS

1. Put the pear pieces in an empty Ninja CREAMi pint container. Let the pear pieces reach the MAX FILL line, then cover it with syrup from the can.
2. Place a storage cover on the container and place it in the freezer for 24 hours.
3. Remove the cover and put the pint in the Ninja CREAMi's outer bowl.
4. Attach the Creamerizer Paddle to the outer bowl's cover.
5. Next, lock the lid by turning it clockwise.
6. Press the "Power" button, then press the "Sorbet" button.
7. Turn the outer bowl and remove it from the machine.
8. Serve right away.

 SHOPPING LIST

- 1 can pears in light syrup

 NUTRITION

Calories: 63

Fat: 0.2g

Carbohydrates: 16.5g

Protein 0.4g
Sodium: 2mg

Fruity Acai Sorbet

DIRECTIONS

1. Combine all necessary ingredients in a blender and blend.
2. Put the mixture in an empty Ninja CREAMi pint container.
3. Place a storage cover on the container and place it in the freezer for 24 hours.
4. Remove the cover and put the pint in the Ninja CREAMi's outer bowl.
5. Attach the Creamerizer Paddle to the outer bowl's cover.
6. Next, lock the lid by turning it clockwise.
7. Press the "Power" button, then press the "Sorbet" button.
8. Turn the outer bowl and remove it from the machine.
9. Serve right away.

 **10 MINUTES**  **4**

SHOPPING LIST

- 1 packet of frozen acai
- ½ cup of blackberries
- ½ cup of banana, peeled and sliced
- ¼ cup of granulated sugar
- 1 cup of water

NUTRITION

Calories: 86

Fat: 0.2g

Carbohydrates: 22.3g

Protein: 0.5g

Sodium: 4mg

Grape Sorbet

 ## DIRECTIONS

1. Combine all necessary ingredients in a blender and blend.
2. Put the mixture in an empty Ninja CREAMi pint container.
3. Place a storage cover on the container and place it in the freezer for 24 hours.
4. Remove the cover and put the pint in the Ninja CREAMi's outer bowl.
5. Attach the Creamerizer Paddle to the outer bowl's cover.
6. Next, lock the lid by turning it clockwise.
7. Press the "Power" button, then press the "Sorbet" button.
8. Turn the outer bowl and remove it from the machine.
9. Serve right away.

15 MINUTES **15 MINUTES** **4**

SHOPPING LIST

- ¾ cup of frozen grape juice concentrate
- 1½ cups of water
- 1 tablespoon of fresh lemon juice

 ## NUTRITION

Calories: 25

Protein: 0.1g

Fat: 0.1g

Carbohydrates: 6.1g

Banana Sorbet

DIRECTIONS

1. Put the banana, water, and caramel sauce in an empty Ninja CREAMi pint container.
2. Place a storage cover on the container and place it in the freezer for 24 hours.
3. Remove the cover and put the pint in the Ninja CREAMi's outer bowl.
4. Attach the Creamerizer Paddle to the outer bowl's cover.
5. Next, lock the lid by turning it clockwise.
6. Press the "Power" button, then press the "Sorbet" button. This process should take up to 2 mins
7. Turn the outer bowl and remove it from the machine.
8. Serve right away.

10 MINUTES

2

SHOPPING LIST

- 1 frozen banana
- 1 teaspoon of cold water
- 2 teaspoons of caramel sauce

NUTRITION

Calories: 70

Fat: 0.2g

Carbohydrates: 18g

Protein 0.7g

Sodium: 25mg

Raspberry Sorbet

INTERMEDIATE RECIPE

 **DIRECTIONS**

1. Combine all necessary ingredients in a blender and blend.
2. Put the mixture in an empty Ninja CREAMi pint container.
3. Place a storage cover on the container and place it in the freezer for 24 hours.
4. Remove the cover and put the pint in the Ninja CREAMi's outer bowl.
5. Attach the Creamerizer Paddle to the outer bowl's cover.
6. Next, lock the lid by turning it clockwise.
7. Press the "Power" button, then press the "Sorbet" button.
8. Turn the outer bowl and remove it from the machine.
9. Serve right away.

10 MINUTES

4

 **SHOPPING**

- 3 cups of fresh raspberries
- ⅓ cup of water
- ⅓ cup of sugar
- ¾ cup of berry punch

NUTRITION

Calories: 135

Carbohydrates: 33.7g

Fat: 0.6g

Protein: 1.1g

Strawberry Sorbet

BASIC RECIPE

 DIRECTIONS

1. Put all the necessary ingredients in an empty Ninja CREAMi pint container.
2. Place a storage cover on the container and place it in the freezer for 24 hours.
3. Remove the cover and put the pint in the Ninja CREAMi's outer bowl.
4. Attach the Creamerizer Paddle to the outer bowl's cover.
5. Next, lock the lid by turning it clockwise.
6. Press the "Power" button, then press the "Sorbet" button.
7. Turn the outer bowl and remove it from the machine.
8. Serve right away.

10 MINUTES

4

 NUTRITION

Calories: 330

Fat 0.1g

Carbohydrates: 72.6g

Protein: 0.1g

 **SHOPPING LIST**

- 6 ounces daiquiri mix
- 2 ounces rum
- ½ cup of frozen strawberries
- ½ cup of simple syrup

Chapter 6

MilkShakes

Cherry Chocolate Milkshake

BASIC RECIPE

 NUTRITION

Calories: 396

Fat: 0.1g

Carbohydrate: 0.5g

Protein 9g

Sodium: 56mg

 SHOPPING LIST

- 1 cup chocolate ice cream
- 1 /2 cup of cherries in syrup drained
- 1/4 Cup of milk

DIRECTIONS

1. Put all the necessary ingredients in an empty Ninja CREAMi pint container.
2. Put the pint in the Ninja CREAMi's outer bowl.
3. Attach the Creamerizer Paddle to the outer bowl's cover.
4. Next, lock the lid by turning it clockwise.
5. Press the "Power" button, then press the "Milkshake" button.
6. Turn the outer bowl and remove it from the machine.
7. Serve right away.

5 MINUTES

5 MINUTES

4

Dulce De Leche Milkshake

BASIC RECIPE

NUTRITION

Calories: 276

Fat: 6g

Carbohydrate: 48g

Protein 7g

Sodium: 530mg

DIRECTIONS

1. Put all the necessary ingredients in an empty Ninja CREAMi pint container.
2. Put the pint in the Ninja CREAMi's outer bowl.
3. Attach the Creamerizer Paddle to the outer bowl's cover.
4. Next, lock the lid by turning it clockwise.
5. Press the "Power" button, then press the "Milkshake" button.
6. Turn the outer bowl and remove it from the machine.
7. Serve right away.

SHOPPING LIST

- 1 cup of vanilla or coffee ice cream
- ½ cup of milk
- 2 tablespoons of sweetened condensed milk
- ¼ teaspoon of salt

5 MINUTES

5 MINUTES

2

Chocolate Protein Milkshake

BASIC RECIPE

NUTRITION

Calories: 242

Fat: 4.8g

Carbohydrate: 30.7g

Protein 18.6g

Sodium: 104mg

DIRECTIONS

1. Put the yogurt, protein powder, and milk in an empty Ninja CREAMi pint container.
2. Put the pint in the Ninja CREAMi's outer bowl.
3. Attach the Creamerizer Paddle to the outer bowl's cover.
4. Next, lock the lid by turning it clockwise.
5. Press the "Power" button, then press the "Milkshake" button.
6. Turn the outer bowl and remove it from the machine.
7. Serve right away.

SHOPPING LIST

• 1 cup of frozen chocolate yogurt
• 1 scoop of chocolate whey protein powder
• 1 cup of whole milk

5 MINUTES

2

Chocolate Ice Cream Milkshake

BASIC RECIPE

 **NUTRITION**

Calories: 279

Fat: 14.5g

Carbohydrate: 29.5g

Protein 7.4g

 SHOPPING LIST

• 1½ cups of chocolate ice cream
• ½ cup of whole milk

 DIRECTIONS

1. Put the ice cream and then milk in an empty Ninja CREAMi pint container.
2. Put the pint in the Ninja CREAMi's outer bowl.
3. Attach the Creamerizer Paddle to the outer bowl's cover.
4. Next, lock the lid by turning it clockwise.
5. Press the "Power" button, then press the "Milkshake" button.
6. Turn the outer bowl and remove it from the machine.
7. Serve right away.

5 MINUTES

1

Mocha Tahini Milkshake

BASIC RECIPE

NUTRITION

Calories: 174
Fat: 11.4g
Carbohydrate: 15.2g

Protein 4.1g

DIRECTIONS

1. Put the ice cream and then milk, tahini, coffee, and fudge in an empty Ninja CREAMi pint container.
2. Put the pint in the Ninja CREAMi's outer bowl.
3. Attach the Creamerizer Paddle to the outer bowl's cover.
4. Next, lock the lid by turning it clockwise.
5. Press the "Power" button, then press the "Milkshake" button.
6. Turn the outer bowl and remove it from the machine.
7. Serve right away.

SHOPPING LIST

- 1½ cups of chocolate ice cream
- ½ cup of unsweetened oat milk
- ¼ cup of tahini
- 2 tablespoons of coffee
- 1 tablespoon of chocolate fudge

5 MINUTES

2

Chocolate Ginger Milkshake

BASIC RECIPE

 **NUTRITION**

Calories: 251

Fat: 12.2g

Carbohydrate: 31.1g

Protein: 4.4g

Sodium: 83mg

 **SHOPPING LIST**

- 1½ cup of chocolate ice cream
- ½ cup of oat milk
- 1 teaspoon of ground ginger
- ¼ cup of chocolate, grated

DIRECTIONS

1. Put the ice cream in an empty Ninja CREAMi pint container.
2. Use a spoon to make a hole in the middle that is 1½-inch wide and extends all the way to the bottom of the pint container. Fill the hole with the remaining ingredients.
3. Put the pint in the Ninja CREAMi's outer bowl.
4. Attach the Creamerizer Paddle to the outer bowl's cover.
5. Next, lock the lid by turning it clockwise.
6. Press the "Power" button, then press the "Milkshake" button.
7. Turn the outer bowl and remove it from the machine.
8. Serve right away.

5 MINUTES

2

Avocado Milkshake

BASIC RECIPE

 ### NUTRITION

Calories: 283
Fat: 15.2g
Carbohydrate: 35.2g

Protein 3.3g
Sodium: 134mg

DIRECTIONS

1. Put the ice cream and then the remaining ingredient in an empty Ninja CREAMi pint container.
2. Put the pint in the Ninja CREAMi's outer bowl.
3. Attach the Creamerizer Paddle to the outer bowl's cover.
4. Next, lock the lid by turning it clockwise.
5. Press the "Power" button, then press the "Milkshake" button.
6. Turn the outer bowl and remove it from the machine.
7. Serve right away.

 ### SHOPPING LIST

- 1 cup of coconut ice cream
- 1 small ripe avocado, peeled, pitted and chopped
- 1 tsp. of fresh lemon juice
- 2 tbsp. of agave nectar
- 1 tsp. of vanilla extract
- Pinch of salt
- ½ cup of oat milk

5 MINUTES

2

Baileys Milkshake

BASIC RECIPE

 **NUTRITION**

Calories: 718

Fat: 22g

Carbohydrate: 85g

Protein 18g

Sodium: 369mg

 SHOPPING LIST

- 1 scoop of vanilla ice cream
- 1 scoop of chocolate ice cream
- 1 tablespoon of chocolate sauce
- 1 tablespoon of caramel sauce
- 2 fluid ounces Baileys Irish Cream
- 1 cup of whole milk

 **DIRECTIONS**

1. Put all the ingredients in an empty Ninja CREAMi pint container.
2. Put the pint in the Ninja CREAMi's outer bowl.

3. Attach the Creamerizer Paddle to the outer bowl's cover.
4. Next, lock the lid by turning it clockwise.
5. Press the "Power" button, then press the "Milkshake" button.
6. Turn the outer bowl and remove it from the machine.
7. Serve right away.

5 MINUTES

5 MINUTES

1

Cashew Butter Milkshake

BASIC RECIPE

NUTRITION

Calories: 297   Protein: 7.4g
Fat: 21.6g
Carbohydrate: 21.1g

DIRECTIONS

1. Put the ice cream in an empty Ninja CREAMi pint container.
2. use a spoon to make a hole in the middle that is 1½-inch wide and extends all the way to the bottom of the pint container. Fill the hole with the remaining ingredients.
3. Put the pint in the Ninja CREAMi's outer bowl.
4. Attach the Creamerizer Paddle to the outer bowl's cover.
5. Next, lock the lid by turning it clockwise.
6. Press the "Power" button, then press the "Milkshake" button.
7. Turn the outer bowl and remove it from the machine.
8. Serve right away.

SHOPPING LIST

- 1½ cups of vanilla ice cream
- ½ cup of canned cashew milk
- ¼ cup of cashew butter

5 MINUTES

2

Pecan Milkshake

BASIC RECIPE

NUTRITION

Calories: 309

Fat: 18.5g

Carbohydrate: 32.6g

Protein 5.6g

SHOPPING LIST

- 1½ cups of vanilla ice cream
- ½ cup of unsweetened soy milk
- 2 tablespoons of maple syrup
- ¼ cup of pecans, chopped
- 1 teaspoon of ground cinnamon
- Pinch of salt

DIRECTIONS

1. Put the ice cream and then soy milk, maple syrup, pecans, cinnamon, and salt in an empty Ninja CREAMi pint container.
2. Put the pint in the Ninja CREAMi's outer bowl.
3. Attach the Creamerizer Paddle to the outer bowl's cover.
4. Next, lock the lid by turning it clockwise.
5. Press the "Power" button, then press the "Milkshake" button.
6. Turn the outer bowl and remove it from the machine.
7. Serve right away.

5 MINUTES

2

Marshmallow Milkshake

BASIC RECIPE

 NUTRITION

Calories: 165

Fat: 6.1g

Carbohydrate: 24.8g

Protein: 3g

SHOPPING LIST

- 1½ cups of vanilla ice cream
- ½ cup of oat milk
- ½ cup of marshmallow cereal

 DIRECTIONS

1. Put the ice cream and then oat milk and marshmallow cereal in an empty Ninja CREAMi pint container.
2. Put the pint in the Ninja CREAMi's outer bowl.
3. Attach the Creamerizer Paddle to the outer bowl's cover.
4. Next, lock the lid by turning it clockwise.
5. Press the "Power" button, then press the "Milkshake" button.
6. Turn the outer bowl and remove it from the machine.
7. Serve right away.

5 MINUTES

2

Orange Milkshake

BASIC RECIPE

 **NUTRITION**

Calories: 346

Fat: 7.8g

Carbohydrate: 62g

Protein: 8g

Sodium: 87.3mg

 **SHOPPING LIST**

- 1 cup of orange juice
- 2 scoops of vanilla ice cream
- ½ cup of milk
- 2 teaspoons of white sugar

DIRECTIONS

1. Put the ice cream, orange juice, milk, and sugar in an empty Ninja CREAMi pint container.
2. Put the pint in the Ninja CREAMi's outer bowl.
3. Attach the Creamerizer Paddle to the outer bowl's cover.
4. Next, lock the lid by turning it clockwise.
5. Press the "Power" button, then press the "Milkshake" button.
6. Turn the outer bowl and remove it from the machine.
7. Serve right away.

5 MINUTES

5 MINUTES

1

Chapter 7

SMOOTHIE BOWLS

Raspberry Smoothie Bowl

INTERMEDIATE RECIPE

SHOPPING LIST

- 1 cup of brewed coffee
- ½ cup of oat milk
- 2 tablespoons of almond butter
- 1 cup of fresh raspberries
- 1 large banana, peeled and sliced

NUTRITION

Calories: 108
Fat: 5.1g
Carbohydrates: 14.9g
Protein: 3g

DIRECTIONS

1. Combine all necessary ingredients in a blender and blend.
2. Put the mixture in an empty Ninja CREAMi pint container.
3. Place a storage cover on the container and place it in the freezer for 24 hours.
4. Remove the cover and put the pint in the Ninja CREAMi's outer bowl.
5. Attach the Creamerizer Paddle to the outer bowl's cover.
6. Next, lock the lid by turning it clockwise.
7. Press the "Power" button, then press the "Smothie Bowl" button.
8. Turn the outer bowl and remove it from the machine.
9. Serve right away.

10 MINUTES

4

Peach & Grapefruit Smoothie Bowl

🧺 SHOPPING LIST

- 1 cup of frozen peach pieces
- 1 cup of vanilla Greek yogurt
- ¼ cup of fresh grapefruit juice
- 2 tbsp. of honey
- ¼ tsp. of vanilla extract
- ½ tsp. of ground cinnamon

📖 NUTRITION

Calories: 193
Fat: 1.7g
Carbohydrates: 35.8g
Protein: 7.9g
Sodium: 87mg

🛍 DIRECTIONS

1. Combine all necessary ingredients in a blender and blend.
2. Put the mixture in an empty Ninja CREAMi pint container.
3. Place a storage cover on the container and place it in the freezer for 24 hours.
4. Remove the cover and put the pint in the Ninja CREAMi's outer bowl.
5. Attach the Creamerizer Paddle to the outer bowl's cover.
6. Next, lock the lid by turning it clockwise.
7. Press the "Power" button, then press the "Smothie Bowl" button.
8. Turn the outer bowl and remove it from the machine.
9. Serve right away.

10 MINUTES

2

Green Fruity Smoothie Bowl

INTERMEDIATE RECIPE

SHOPPING LIST

- 1 banana, peeled and cut into 1-inch pieces
- ½ of avocado, peeled, pitted and cut into 1-inch pieces
- 1 cup of fresh kale leaves
- 1 C. green apple, peeled, cored and cut into 1-inch pieces
- ¼ cup of unsweetened coconut milk
- 2 tbsp. of agave nectar

NUTRITION

Calories: 359
Fat: 17.3g
Carbohydrates: 54.4g
Protein: 3.6g

DIRECTIONS

1. Combine all the necessary ingredients in a blender and blend.
2. Put the mixture in an empty Ninja CREAMi pint container.
3. Place a storage cover on the container and place it in the freezer for 24 hours.
4. Remove the cover and put the pint in the Ninja CREAMi's outer bowl.
5. Attach the Creamerizer Paddle to the outer bowl's cover.
6. Next, lock the lid by turning it clockwise.
7. Press the "Power" button, then press the "Smoothie Bowl" button.
8. Turn the outer bowl and remove it from the machine.
9. Serve right away.

10 MINUTES

2

Piña Colada Smoothie Bowl

INTERMEDIATE RECIPE

🧺 SHOPPING LIST

- 1½ cups of canned pineapple chunks in their juice
- ½ cup of canned coconut milk
- 1 tablespoon of agave nectar

📖 NUTRITION

Calories: 359

Fat: 17.3g

Carbohydrates: 54.4g

Protein: 3.6g

🛍️ DIRECTIONS

1. Put the pineapple chunks, coconut milk, and agave in an empty Ninja CREAMi pint container.
2. Place a storage cover on the container and place it in the freezer for 24 hours.
3. Remove the cover and put the pint in the Ninja CREAMi's outer bowl.
4. Attach the Creamerizer Paddle to the outer bowl's cover.
5. Next, lock the lid by turning it clockwise.
6. Press the "Power" button, then press the "Smoothie Bowl" button.
7. Turn the outer bowl and remove it from the machine.
8. Serve right away.

10 MINUTES

4

Frozen Fruit Smoothie Bowl

INTERMEDIATE RECIPE

🧺 SHOPPING LIST

- 1 ripe banana, peeled and cut in 1-inch pieces
- 2 cup of frozen fruit mix
- 1¼ cup of vanilla yogurt

📖 NUTRITION

Calories: 251

Fat: 2.1g

Carbohydrates: 45.2g

Protein: 10.8g

Sodium: 108mg

🛍 DIRECTIONS

1. Combine all the necessary ingredients in a blender and blend.
2. Put the mixture in an empty Ninja CREAMi pint container.
3. Place a storage cover on the container and place it in the freezer for 24 hours.
4. Remove the cover and put the pint in the Ninja CREAMi's outer bowl.
5. Attach the Creamerizer Paddle to the outer bowl's cover.
6. Next, lock the lid by turning it clockwise.
7. Press the "Power" button, then press the "Smoothie Bowl" button.
8. Turn the outer bowl and remove it from the machine.
9. Serve right away.

10 MINUTES

2

Mango & Orange Smoothie Bowl

INTERMEDIATE RECIPE

🧺 SHOPPING LIST

- 1 cup of frozen mango chunks
- 1 cup of plain whole milk yogurt
- ¼ cup of fresh orange juice
- 2 tablespoons of maple syrup
- ½ teaspoon of ground turmeric
- 1/8 teaspoon of ground cinnamon
- 1/8 teaspoon of ground ginger
- Pinch of ground black pepper

📖 NUTRITION

Calories: 188

Fat: 4.2g

Carbohydrates: 34.8g

Protein: 4.9g

🛍 DIRECTIONS

1. Combine all the necessary ingredients in a blender and blend.
2. Put the mixture in an empty Ninja CREAMi pint container.
3. Place a storage cover on the container and place it in the freezer for 24 hours.
4. Remove the cover and put the pint in the Ninja CREAMi's outer bowl.
5. Attach the Creamerizer Paddle to the outer bowl's cover.
6. Next, lock the lid by turning it clockwise.
7. Press the "Power" button, then press the "Smothie Bowl" button.
8. Turn the outer bowl and remove it from the machine.
9. Serve right away.

10 MINUTES

2

Fruity Coffee Smoothie Bowl

INTERMEDIATE RECIPE

SHOPPING LIST

- 1 cup of brewed coffee
- ½ cup of oat milk
- 2 tbsp. of almond butter
- 1 cup of fresh raspberries
- 1 large banana, peeled and sliced

NUTRITION

Calories: 108

Fat: 5.1g

Carbohydrates: 14.9g

Protein: 3g

Sodium: 84mg

DIRECTIONS

1. Combine all the necessary ingredients in a blender and blend.
2. Put the mixture in an empty Ninja CREAMi pint container.
3. Place a storage cover on the container and place it in the freezer for 24 hours.
4. Remove the cover and put the pint in the Ninja CREAMi's outer bowl.
5. Attach the Creamerizer Paddle to the outer bowl's cover.
6. Next, lock the lid by turning it clockwise.
7. Press the "Power" button, then press the "Smothie Bowl" button.
8. Turn the outer bowl and remove it from the machine.
9. Serve right away.

10
MINUTES

4

Three Fruit Smoothie Bowl

SHOPPING LIST

- 1 cup of frozen dragon fruit pieces
- ¾ cup of fresh strawberries, hulled and quartered
- ¾ cup of pineapple, cut in 1-inch pieces
- ½ cup of low-fat plain yogurt
- 2 tbsp. of agave nectar
- 1 tbsp. of fresh lime juice

NUTRITION

Calories: 183

Fat: 1.2g

Carbohydrates: 40.5g

Protein: 4.5g

Sodium: 94mg

DIRECTIONS

1. Combine all the necessary ingredients in a blender and blend.
2. Put the mixture in an empty Ninja CREAMi pint container.
3. Place a storage cover on the container and place it in the freezer for 24 hours.
4. Remove the cover and put the pint in the Ninja CREAMi's outer bowl.
5. Attach the Creamerizer Paddle to the outer bowl's cover.
6. Next, lock the lid by turning it clockwise.
7. Press the "Power" button, then press the "Smothie Bowl" button.
8. Turn the outer bowl and remove it from the machine.
9. Serve right away.

10 MINUTES

2

Strawberry-orange Creme Smoothie

INTERMEDIATE RECIPE

🧺 SHOPPING LIST

- 1 container Yoplait Greek 100 orange creme yogurt
- ½ cup of fresh strawberries, hulled
- ¼ cup of ice cubes (optional)
- ¼ cup of orange juice

📖 NUTRITION

Calories: 136

Fat: 0.3g

Carbohydrates: 20g

Protein: 12g

Sodium: 103mg

🛍️ DIRECTIONS

1. Put all the necessary ingredients in an empty Ninja CREAMi pint container.
2. Put the pint in the Ninja CREAMi's outer bowl.
3. Next, lock the lid by turning it clockwise.
4. Press the "Power" button, then press the "Smoothie" button.
5. Turn the outer bowl and remove it from the machine.
6. Serve right away.

10 MINUTES

1

Vanilla Pumpkin Pie Smoothie

INTERMEDIATE RECIPE

🧺 SHOPPING LIST

- 4 ounces pumpkin pie filling (such as Libby's)
- ½ cup of vanilla frozen yogurt
- ¼ cup of ice
- ¼ cup of vanilla-flavored soy milk
- ½ teaspoon of ground cinnamon
- 1 pinch of ground nutmeg
- ⅛ teaspoon of vanilla extract

📖 NUTRITION

Calories: 260

Fat: 4.8g

Carbohydrates: 50g

Protein: 5.6g

Sodium: 329mg

🛍 DIRECTIONS

1. Combine the frozen yogurt, pumpkin pie filling, soy milk, cinnamon, ice, nutmeg, and vanilla extract in an empty Ninja CREAMi pint container.
2. Put the pint in the Ninja CREAMi's outer bowl.
3. Next, lock the lid by turning it clockwise.
4. Press the "Power" button, then press the "Smothie" button.
5. Turn the outer bowl and remove it from the machine.
6. Serve right away.

10 MINUTES

1

Kale, Avocado & Fruit Smoothie Bowl

INTERMEDIATE RECIPE

SHOPPING LIST

- 1 banana, peeled and cut into 1-inch pieces
- ½ of avocado, peeled, pitted and cut into 1-inch pieces
- 1 cup of fresh kale leaves
- 1 cup of green apple, peeled, cored and cut into 1-inch pieces
- ¼ cup of unsweetened coconut milk
- 2 tablespoons of agave nectar

NUTRITION

Calories: 179

Fat: 8.7g

Carbohydrates: 27.2g

Protein: 1.8g

DIRECTIONS

1. Combine all the necessary ingredients in a blender and blend.
2. Put the mixture in an empty Ninja CREAMi pint container.
3. Place a storage cover on the container and place it in the freezer for 24 hours.
4. Remove the cover and put the pint in the Ninja CREAMi's outer bowl.
5. Attach the Creamerizer Paddle to the outer bowl's cover.
6. Next, lock the lid by turning it clockwise.
7. Press the "Power" button, then press the "Smothie Bowl" button.
8. Turn the outer bowl and remove it from the machine.
9. Serve right away.

10 MINUTES

4

Recipes Index

Made in the USA
Monee, IL
30 June 2023